INTRODUCTION

Of all the popular pets, the rabbit is perhaps the one most associated with qualities of beauty and gentleness. In folklore and children's books, the rabbit is the animal nearly always portrayed as being cute and friendly—the benign hero that is rarely evil. Most adults who owned a rabbit than a pet. But with the development of breeds, and a range of coat colors, came the hobby of rabbit keeping for the sheer fun and love of doing so.

Today, the rabbit is seen in more varieties than ever before. There is a bewildering array of colors, coat patterns, and fur

Rabbits don't have to be purebred to be beautiful and gentle pets. Rabbits are natural pets for children because many children's books and comic characters portray rabbits as heroes.

at some stage during their childhood will attest to the fact that these are very lovable and undemanding little pets.

The rabbit has retained its popularity over many centuries. It is one of the major four mammals—the others being dogs, cats, and mice—whose popularity can be traced back to the earliest civilizations. In those far-off days, the rabbit was essentially a food item, rather types. A rabbit can sport long, normal, or short ears. In size, it can range from a diminutive dwarf to a giant breed larger than some small dogs.

Until very recent times, rabbits were generally regarded as outdoor pets. This has changed dramatically in recent years with the availability of easily cleaned indoor cages designed with this purpose in mind. Indeed, rabbit owners of past years would be amazed at just what is available for these pets.

Apart from clubs for each of the breeds, there are rabbit magazines, videos on their care, stock management systems, all kinds of feeding utensils, commercially produced bedding and cage litters, special foods and tonics—even harnesses so that you can leash train your little pet. In the area of collectibles there is pottery, paintings, stamps, jewelry, clothing, stationery, and garden ornaments, to name but a few. The cute little bunny is seemingly everywhere.

You can join your nearest rabbit club, and there is a vast network of rabbit shows for the real enthusiast to visit or compete in.

In this small guidebook, you will find all the information that you need to get started in this hobby, either as a one-bunny owner, an exhibitor, or a potential breeder.

BRIEF RABBIT HISTORY

It is generally accepted that the domestic rabbit was developed from the species *Oryctolagus cuniculus,* which was native to southern France, Spain, Portugal, and possibly North Africa. It is from Spain that the species was taken to other countries, first by the Phoenicians, and later by the Romans. Rabbits were kept as a prime source of meat.

The Normans are credited with introducing rabbits to Britain, whose explorers took them to many other countries as the British Empire grew. Other European empire builders, such as the Spanish, French, and Dutch, also transported rabbits in order to create food and game sources in lands where the rabbit previously was not seen.

Rabbits originated in southern France, Spain, Portugal, and perhaps even North Africa. They are scientifically known as *Oryctolagus cuniculus.*

Through human intervention, this single species was introduced to most countries of the world. The rabbit proved prolific in many such countries. The more so if, as in Australia, there were few natural predators to keep population growth in check. It is now considered that, in most instances, these introductions proved to be a disaster in the

Over the centuries that they have been kept in captivity, rabbits have been developed in most colors in which other animals are found, but they have also developed special varieties that have long, drooping ears. Rabbits with drooping ears are called lops.

Rabbits are found in many coat (fur) colors and textures. There are long-haired rabbits which we know as woolly breeds such as Angoras. There are also rabbits with very fine coats and these may be referred to as satins.

damage and interference they created for the indigenous species of flora and fauna.

It is not known for sure when the domestic rabbit was introduced to the US. It is probable that early European migrants took rabbits with them. But not until the 1900s did the rabbit hobby really begin to take off—in the form of the Belgian Hare, which is a rabbit breed, not a hare.

THE DOMESTIC RABBIT

Although captive rabbits were no doubt kept as pets from the time we humans started to keep them as a food source, it was not until much later that truly domesticated strains started to appear. These became established once breeders, in particular European

Skeleton of a medium-sized rabbit. Note the length of the hind legs, which accounts for the rabbit's hippity-hop gait.

monks, began to retain rabbits in small enclosures and hutches. This enabled any mutations that arrived to survive and be propagated.

Tracing the history of the various breeds is almost impossible, but we do know that certain color types, such as the albino, blue, brown, and yellow, were known prior to the 1700s. In the following 150 years, the English, Himalayan, Angora, and

many other breeds had become established.

Thereafter, matters become very confusing. By the mid-19th Century, rabbit breeding was a very popular pastime. The first shows were being held. Very similar rabbits in each European country were being given different names. Breeds rose and declined in popularity, only to appear again under a different name some years later.

ZOOLOGICAL STANDING

The rabbit was originally thought to be a rodent and was placed in the order Rodentia by most authorities. Today the rabbit is not regarded as a close relative of the rodents and appears in the order Lagomorpha. One of the important differences between rabbits and rodents is that rabbits have paired upper incisors, meaning that there is one tooth behind another. In rodents, the incisors are single.

Lagomorpha is divided into two families. Ochotonidae contains the pikas, mouse hares, or conies. Leporidae houses the rabbits and hares, of which there are 47 species. These are distributed throughout the world with the exception of the West Indies, Madagascar, the southern-most areas of South America, and many oceanic islands.

The jack rabbit and snowshoe rabbit of the US are actually hares—the cottontails and the western pygmy rabbit being the true rabbits of North America. Distinction between hares and rabbits is based on a number of features. Anatomically, hares are normally larger, have black tips to their ears, and have distinctive palate bones when compared to rabbits.

Hares do not live in burrows, but in shallow depressions. Their young are not born in nests. They are born fully furred with eyes open. Within minutes of birth, they are able to run. Rabbits are born in a lined nest within a burrow, are blind, deaf, naked, and quite helpless for a number of days. There are 24 rabbit species, the cottontails accounting for 13 of them. As far as is known, all domestic rabbit breeds were developed from the single species discussed earlier.

THE MEANING OF NAMES

As a final note, an explanation of the scientific names that are applied to rabbits may be of interest.

Lagomorpha: *Lago* is derived from the Greek word for hare; *morpho* means form. Thus, the name means a kind of hare.

Oryctolagus: *Orycto* is Greek, meaning a dugout or digger. *Lagus* is hare. Thus, the meaning is a digging hare (a rabbit).

cuniculus: This is Latin meaning an underground passage, or a rabbit.

The use of Greek and Latin in scientific nomenclature derives from the fact that they were the languages of scholars. Scientific names are accepted internationally. They are the same in every language—a useful benefit. No two species ever have the same binomial scientific name, whereas a species may have one or many common names in a given language. This can and does create confusion.

There are 24 species of rabbit, with the cottontails accounting for 13 of the 24. The long-eared rabbits, like the one shown here, were developed from the same species as the lop, or droop-eared variety, shown on the facing page.

There are several lop-eared breeds of rabbit. All, of course, have drooping ears, though some are longer than others. There is the English Lop, the French Lop, the Mini (Dwarf) Lop, the Holland (Dutch) Lop, and the American Fuzzy Lop.

CHOOSING YOUR RABBIT

Unfortunately, many pet owners purchase their new companions on an impulse. This is the worst way to obtain a pet. It accounts for a large percentage of the millions of abandoned or uncared for pets.

You should not assume that rabbits are suited to your needs—another little critter, such as a hamster, mouse, or hedgehog, may be a better choice. When selecting a pet, you must consider why you want that particular animal, rather than others. Do not assume that there are no drawbacks. Indeed, these are what you should focus on before all else.

Having decided the rabbit is the pet for you, there are still many factors involved in making the *right* choice. Rabbits come in many varieties and sizes. You must obtain housing suited to the size of the pet. There are many kinds of housing. Which is best for you? In this chapter, we will look at *all* of the important considerations. Due reflection on them will dramatically increase the possibility that you will be happy with your pet. In turn, this will mean that the little bunny will have a very good home.

IS A RABBIT THE RIGHT CHOICE?

As with any pet, the first thing to be said is that when you obtain a rabbit, it should be a

Rabbits are categorized by size, ear length, coat characteristics, and color. This lovely rabbit is called the English Spot.

Many rabbits have coats and colors which look like well-known rabbit varieties, but they lack the purebred genetic background. This means that even if a rabbit looks like an English Spot, it probably won't produce English Spot offspring unless its parents were English Spots.

commitment for its entire life. It should not be a five-minute wonder that becomes neglected once the initial novelty wears off. Rabbits are not intelligent like dogs, cats, or parrots. They can respond to your voice, and they do get to know their owner. But you cannot train them to the level of these other pets.

They can be litter box trained, but don't assume this will be to the same standard as a dog or cat, or achieved with such ease. They can be lead trained, but not like a dog. Nor can they be left to wander around your garden without supervision at all times.

Baby bunnies are adorable, but when they grow up will you still be as keen on them? Never purchase a rabbit for a small child unless *you* want one. Many children lose interest in pets once they own them. You must accept total responsibility for the welfare of the rabbit. If it becomes ill, can you afford veterinary attention? If not, neither a rabbit nor any other pet should be obtained. If you are not fastidious in cleaning your rabbit's accommodations, they will smell—have no illusions on this account.

CHOICE OF BREED

The breed you decide upon should reflect your circumstances. If the rabbit is to live indoors, one of the smaller breeds may be the better choice. They will also be less costly to feed. They will not need as much space as the large breeds, and there will be less fecal matter and urine to contend with. Although

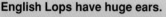
English Lops have huge ears.

This young mixed-breed rabbit is ready to go to its new home. Rabbits should never be purchased before the age of eight to ten weeks.

the Angora (longhaired) breeds look magnificent when they are seen at shows, they are not the best choice for households in which there are small children. Further, unless you are prepared to devote regular time to grooming, that long woolly coat will soon become a mass of tangles and mats. Children may put sticky sweets and other objects in the fur, so do think carefully about these practical aspects.

The lops are another example of breeds suited only to those who can devote extra attention to their pets. The ears can dangle into bowls of water, soon collecting dust and food on the damp fur. They are more prone to ear mites and cuts than the natural erect ear of typical rabbits.

The average pet owner is advised to restrict his choice to the medium-to-small breeds that are easy to care for and low cost in upkeep.

HOUSING

This topic is discussed in its own chapter. Here it need only be said that the indoor rabbit home will be less costly than that for the outdoor pet. The latter needs to be more rugged in its construction to provide good insulation against both extremes of cold and heat, as well as being waterproof.

PURCHASE AGE

For most purposes it is usually better to obtain a young rabbit. It will have the whole of its life with you, and baby rabbits are very cute and playful. If you plan to be a breeder or exhibitor, there is merit in obtaining young adults. Their quality can be better assessed.

Rabbits are normally weaned when they are four to six weeks of age. However, it is recommended that you wait until the youngsters are eight to ten weeks old before obtaining them. The extra two or more weeks enables these recently weaned babies to become very independent of their mother. Also, they will be better able to cope with the high stress factor that is inherent when any young animal leaves its mother and siblings to transfer to a new home.

Most problems that pet owners experience with young rabbits—indeed any mammal—is that they obtain babies that are too young. Within days, the babies react negatively to the change of environment. The stress prompts minor conditions, evident in the form of diarrhea. These conditions may develop rapidly into major problems at a time when the youngster's developing immune system is at its most vulnerable. This aspect cannot be overstressed.

CHOICE OF SEX

The male rabbit is called a buck; the female is called a doe. Either will make a fine pet. Females will usually cohabit with each other without undue problems—males will tend to fight once mature.

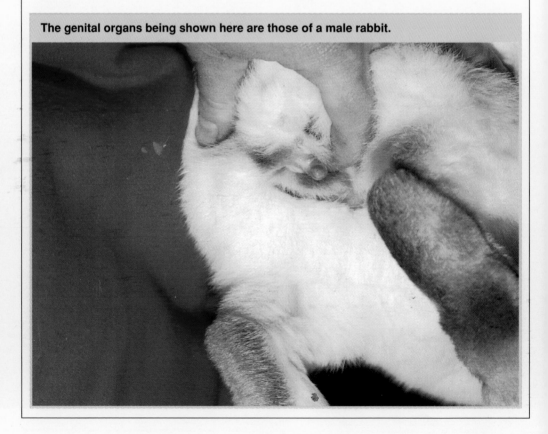
The genital organs being shown here are those of a male rabbit.

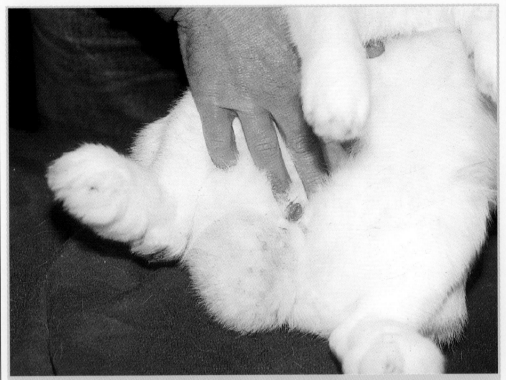

The genital organs pictured here are those of a female rabbit.

These are general guidelines. If males are reared together from babies, and have spacious accommodations, they may become big friends—as long as no females are scented nearby. If you want to keep a buck and doe together, have them neutered. They will live in harmony without the downside of unwanted litters. In fact, it is advisable to have any pet rabbit neutered: This is responsible ownership. The simple surgery can be done when the babies are about three to four months old.

TOTAL HOBBY COST

Before you purchase your new pet, it is wise to determine what the total cost will be based on the breed that you want, and its cage or hutch—these two things being the two major start-up costs. The advantage of this is that if you find that it is more than you estimated, it would be prudent to wait the extra few weeks. This way, you do not have to economize and maybe settle for a smaller and less suitable rabbit home, nor have to change your choice of breed for a lower cost mixed-breed pet.

WHERE TO BUY

Pet shops carry a variety of rabbit breeds. Additionally, they are one-stop shopping places for all of your pet-related needs—hutch, food, bedding, etc.

Your first considerations are that the premises are clean, there is no undue smell, and the conditions under which the pets are kept are satisfactory—spacious, clean, with food and water pots present.

Keep in mind that a pet shop cannot stock every breed of rabbit. If you have your heart set on one of the more uncommon breeds, you may have to travel out of your area in order to obtain it.

Do not purchase rabbits from open markets (they may pose a health risk) or any other source where the seller cannot provide you with good after-sales service.

HEALTH AND TEMPERAMENT

Ahead of any other considerations when purchasing your rabbit are health and temperament. If these are not as they should be, you start at a considerable disadvantage, and things could go downhill.

Young rabbits can rapidly deteriorate if they are not in the best of health when you obtain them. Look for the following signs of ill health: cloudy or weeping eyes, runny nose, or nostrils that are swollen, and ears that display signs of wax in them, and/or have a foul odor. There should be no swellings on the body of the rabbit, no bald or sore spots, and no signs of parasites. Fleas leave characteristic dark specks in the fur and move quickly when the fur is brushed against its lie. Mites move more slowly and are a gray color.

If a rabbit has wet front feet, this is a bad sign. It is usually the result of continual wiping of a runny nose—the condition being known as snuffles. It could prove dangerous, even fatal. Inspect the anal region for signs of diarrhea (stained fur) or compacted fecal matter.

The fur should never look dry or lackluster. Finally, any rabbit that looks unusually lethargic or retreats when approached has a problem.

With regard to temperament, any young rabbit should display no fear of humans, nor any reluctance at being handled. Attempts to scratch or bite indicate either a very nervous disposition or fear derived from lack of handling by the breeder when the rabbit was a baby. This assumes that the rabbit is handled correctly: any animal will display resistance if it is picked up in a way that it causes fear or pain.

PURCHASE DO'S AND DON'TS

1. Do be sure that a rabbit is the right pet for you.

2. Do review the breeds for best-size choice.

3. Do not select a breed that requires extra care if your time is limited.

4. Do not purchase a bunny on an impulse, especially for a child.

5. Do check breed, housing, and other costs beforehand so that you do not have to compromise on these expenditures.

6. Do not purchase any rabbit that looks ill, or cannot be handled with ease.

7. Do have pet rabbits neutered.

BEFORE you buy your pet rabbit, you must decide about where it will live (inside the house or outside in a hutch). This is often predicated on the size to which it will eventually grow. That's the problem with buying an unknown breed of rabbit. You won't know how large it will be when it matures.

HOUSING

A rabbit can live in your home, in an outdoor building, or in your yard. Each presents its own special needs when related to the actual housing. It is *crucially* important that these differences are considered. If not, you may be subjecting your pet to a very miserable existence when it is in its little home.

Outdoor hutch: This must be well constructed so that it is protected from adverse weather—snow, rain, cold winds, dampness, and excessive heat. It must also be protected from predators.

Outbuilding hutch: This will be protected from inclement weather but must still be cozy if there is no heating in the building. If the building is heated—as in a breeding room—you can use the same kind of hutch, or cage, that you would use for the house rabbit.

The house cage: This needs minimal protection from the environment, its main features being that it can be readily cleaned and provides a comfortable place of retreat for the rabbit.

Let us look at these varying needs in terms of their general design and the materials from which they are made.

THE OUTDOOR HUTCH

Traditionally, hutches were made of wood and wire. Today, all-wire hutches are available, and

Outside rabbit hutches or pens must be strong enough to keep the rabbit in and predators (dogs, cats, snakes, etc.) out.

The inside of the hutch must be clean, dry and contain suitable bedding. It must also contain space for exercising, feeding and sleeping.

they are the best choice for outdoors: your pet shop may stock them, or can special order one for you in a range of styles and prices. It is important that the roof overhangs the side walls, is waterproofed, and sloped so that rain water can drain away. It should be raised from the ground for good floor ventilation and to deny rodents a hiding place. Double side walls, with insulation between them, are certainly needed in areas with very cold winters, or hot summers.

There should be an exercise/feeding area leading to a darkened sleeping box. The exercise area will have a weldwire front, preferably epoxy coated for ease of cleaning, and to prevent rust. This front panel should be removable or hinged to facilitate easy cleaning of the hutch. Above the floor can be a raised small-holed weldwire mesh so that fecal matter can drop through this to the floor, or onto a removable litter tray.

It is important that mesh floors are small holed. Otherwise, they will be uncomfortable, possibly even dangerous, to the feet of your pet. A more recent innovation is the use of thin, epoxy-coated bars sufficiently spaced to allow fecal matter to fall between them, yet which are easy to clean and more comfortable for the rabbit's feet.

If you do not like mesh floors, a laminated or plastic-coated timber will make cleaning much easier and reduce the potential for urine to soak into the wood, creating odors. The outdoor hutch should be positioned facing south so that it enjoys the early morning sun and is protected from cold northerly winds.

You can screen it with conifers or fencing to provide extra weather protection and create a more aesthetically pleasing appearance. If the hutch is placed under an overhang of some kind, it will provide even more protection and will make regular cleaning chores much easier when it is raining or windy.

THE INDOOR HUTCH

Pet shops will have a selection of indoor hutches and cages from which to choose. Today, the use of metal and galvanized weldwire cages has largely replaced the wooden indoor hutch for a number of reasons.

They are longer lasting, easier to keep clean, create less odors than unprotected low-cost wooden hutches, provide total ventilation, offer maximum viewing for you and the rabbit, and provide minimal potential for pathogenic (disease-causing) organisms to create colonies. Those that are epoxy coated are the best. They are suggested for in-home use, and they look better.

All-metal cages may be fitted with external nestboxes to provide the needed cozy bedroom retreat, or the nestbox can be placed within the cage. These modern cages can be raised on attachable legs and can be stacked to maximize space use for breeders. They come in a range of sizes and

It is possible to keep more than one rabbit in a given area, but keep in mind that rabbits can be aggressive during their breeding cycle.

This lovely English Angora is kept inside the house in a suitable cage. Pet shops have many small animal cages offered for sale.

may have pull-out trays for ease of cleaning.

Tiered cages can be placed on wheels to make moving them easy—a decided benefit in a breeding room, or in your home when you need to clean behind them.

CAGE OR HUTCH SIZE

The factors that you need to take into account when deciding on the size of your rabbit's home are:

1. The breed of rabbit. Large breeds, such as the Flemish Giant, Checkered Giant, or Chinchilla, will clearly need a large home when compared to the smaller breeds, like the Dutch, the mini breeds, and the Netherland Dwarf.

2. Accommodations housing two rabbits should be about one-third larger than if they were housing a single occupant.

3. If the pet will be given plenty of time out of its cage to roam freely in a room or a penned exercise area, the cage is only a retreat and sleeping area: It can be minimal in size. The more time the pet must spend in its home, the greater the home should be in size.

As a general guide, work on the following basis. If the rabbit is restricted to its home most of the day, the cage length should be about 3-4 times the length of the adult rabbit, its width twice the rabbit's length. No rabbit should *ever* be denied a reasonable amount of time to exercise, which

Before you buy a rabbit, you must be sure of its pedigree and its tolerance to human handling. That's why you should buy your rabbit ONLY at a pet shop. Some farmers grow rabbits for food. Their rabbits are almost never handled, are not tame, and their genetic background is also questionable.

means to run, outside of its cage or hutch. Breeders should provide such facility via special enclosures (indoor and/or outdoor depending on the weather) that their stock can spend some time in each week.

FLOOR COVERING

Hutches and cages with wooden floors can be covered with wood shavings, large bags of commercial white pine being an economical choice. Do *not*

ultimately reduces the rabbit's potential life span.

You can place plain paper sheets under the shavings, or use just the paper as the base. Fresh hay can be used in the nestbox. Supply an ample amount because the rabbit will eat it. Granulated and shredded paper are other possibilities for floor-covering material. Avoid straw: its ends can be sharp and potentially dangerous, apart from its having virtually no absorbency.

Flemish Giants are large rabbits that were originally developed as food animals. Rabbit meat is still a popular dish in Belgium, France, and many other areas.

use cedar shavings for the floor. The high phenol content makes it very dangerous to small mammals. It is illegal for small pets in some states for this reason. It adversely affects the respiratory system, slows down the immune system, and

Plain or newsprint paper can be used in trays beneath mesh floors. They will protect the base from urine staining. In outdoor hutches with mesh floors, you are advised to feature epoxy-coated weldwire so that the floor is not as cold or frosty during the winter months. It would be worthwhile having an attachable thermoplastic cover panel for such cages during very cold weather: Be sure to provide ventilation holes along the top edge of it.

ROUTINE CLEANING

It is very important that your rabbit's home is thoroughly cleaned at least once a week—more often if it starts to smell. Rabbits are odor free: it is the ammonium compounds in their urine and fecal matter that smell. Keep the disposal of your pet's waste matter under control and you eliminate unpleasant odors. Always bear in mind that, as a pet owner, you can become unaware of mild odors, but visitors may smell them instantly!

Scented aerosols and their like are not the answer to odors; they merely mask them temporarily. The remedy is regular cleaning and constant removal of the source: fecal matter, urine-soaked bedding, and uneaten fresh food. Ask at your pet shop for an odor *neutralizer*. These formulations change the chemical structure of the odorous ammonium compounds into a non-smelly compound. You can use them if a carpet or other odor-absorbent material is accidentally soiled by a pet.

Household bleach diluted in water is recommended for periodic cleaning, but be sure it is thoroughly rinsed with water after cleaning has been completed. This removes residual compounds that might be dangerous. Do not use concentrated disinfectants because you think that they will be more effective as anti-parasitic and anti-bacterial agents. They are just as effective in the diluted form.

Cleaning should not be restricted to the floor and/or tray but should also include the cage bars, feeding utensils, and everything else in the cage, especially the nestbox. Both odors and pathogens can build up only if they have a surface on, or in, which they can remain undisturbed. Cracks and crevices are such places. Never leave soiled floor-covering material near the cage: dispose of it as soon as possible, especially if you are a breeder with a number of rabbits. Always remember that if your pet's home smells, it is a direct reflection of your lack of cleaning, not the fault of the pet. He or she no more likes to live in such a home than you do.

HOUSING DO'S AND DON'TS

1. Do not skimp on your pet's housing—obtain the best available from your pet store. It will be worth it in the long run.

2. Be sure that your rabbit's home reflects its environment. An outdoor hutch must be more robust than its indoor equivalent.

3. Ensure that the home is large enough for the breed that you have selected.

4. Do not leave wooden floors unprotected from urine staining. They will quickly start to smell.

5. Attend to routine cleaning on a regular basis—daily if it is needed.

English Angoras were developed for their long soft coats. Their fur is used for fancy ladies' sweaters and other articles of clothing.

THE HOUSE RABBIT

Never before has the concept of keeping a rabbit in the home been more popular than today. Matters have been helped with the availability of cages better suited to a home than were the wooden hutches of former years, which were much more difficult to keep odor free.

The growing number of small and mini breeds has given further impetus to the desire to keep a pet rabbit in the home, rather than its being kept outdoors or in a shed. The opportunity for pet and owner to interact is more restricted if the pet is not very accessible, and part of the owner's home life.

Once a rabbit is given ample room in which to move about as nature intended, you will find that it is a totally different pet from the one that sits hunched up in a cage for the greater part of its life. In a home situation, it is more active, playful, and confiding. It is able to display its full character.

IMPORTANT CONSIDERATIONS

If you are thinking of keeping a pet bunny in your home, you will want to know about the negatives, and how they can be overcome, or at least minimized to an acceptable level. The first thing to be said is that if you think you can train a rabbit to be as clean in its toiletry habits as a cat or dog, you will be disappointed.

This does not mean that it can't be litter box trained; it is a case

The Mini Lop is a solid, thickset little rabbit with broad shoulders. It is among the more popular lop-type rabbits.

Pet shops have small rabbits and large rabbits. Of course the small rabbits don't stay small for long! Unsold bunnies grow into breeding–size rabbits and are usually more expensive than the young bunnies. The advantage of buying a fully grown rabbit is that you won't have to guess about how large it will be.

that it will never be 100 percent. The reason lies in the difference between dogs and cats, which are carnivores, and rabbits, which are herbivores. Carnivores eat a large amount of food at a single meal. Then they rest for a few hours to digest the food. The unwanted fecal matter is then expelled. They can be trained to deposit their fecal matter in a given spot or do it outdoors, both because they are more intelligent, and because their toiletry needs are spaced over a number of hours. You get more warning and can react appropriately.

The rabbit is a constant browser. Food is continually passing through the digestive system and leaving at the other end. While a rabbit will tend to use the same spot most of the time, this is not a fastidious routine: it will defecate where and when nature suggests it is "time."

Further, not all voided pellets are fecal matter: some are partially digested foods that the rabbit will eat. They are called cecal pellets.

There are other considerations to be kept in mind if your pet is to be a house rabbit. Rabbits will eat or nibble any vegetable matter that is within reach, including house plants. If they are not supplied with ample materials on which to keep their teeth in trim, they may use any appropriate wood, as in furniture, to achieve this. Give them items such as wooden cotton bobbins, cardboard rolls, and fruit tree branches to play with.

Being very inquisitive, they may nibble on electrical wire if it is not neatly hidden, or protected in appropriate casing.

You must ensure that doors leading to the outdoors are kept closed. If your pet wanders outside, it may fall victim to a passing dog or cat. It may easily get lost as it meanders under bushes nibbling at grass and other delicacies—including your cherished flowers—that it finds.

No pet is without some drawbacks when kept as a home companion and given reasonable freedom. You must balance the many benefits against the negatives, or inconveniences, to you. One thing that is most important for you to understand is that you cannot train a rabbit by using discipline on it as you might a dog or cat. If you are the kind with a short fuse, forget having a house rabbit—you, not the bunny, would be the major problem!

OVERCOMING PROBLEMS

Now that you understand the potential problems, let us see how they can be overcome, or minimized. You have various options.

1. The rabbit can be kept in the house but restricted to a given room, such as an enclosed patio. There it can be given freedom to exercise. Choose a place that is not carpeted, thus more easily kept clean.

2. If space permits, you can keep the bunny in a pen complete with a nestbox for its sleeping place. This gives it more freedom than a cage but restricts the area in which it can wander around. You can give it full-room freedom when you are there to supervise its activities.

3. You can litter box train it, allowing freedom in those rooms in which litter boxes are kept. This will minimize fecal problems.

4. If you have an unused spare room, you can make it your pet's room, furnishing it with a cage, logs, rocks, and other things to make life generally interesting. This set-up would be better for two or more rabbits because they will play and keep each other company when you are not with them.

LITTER BOX TRAINING

Many people fail to litter box train their pets because they lack patience or because they go about it the wrong way. With rabbits, patience and method are vital prerequisites. The following are basic guidelines to utilize.

1. Purchase a litter box appropriate for the size of your bunny. Your pet must be able to hop into the box without problems, and be able to turn around in it. Ideally, the cage will be large enough to hold the litter box and still leave room for the pet to eat and sleep. If not, use guideline 2.

The litter material can be granulated paper, shavings, paper sheets, or commercial wood fiber and similar biodegradable litters. Avoid silicon clay cat litters, which can be dangerous to your pet's health.

2. Give the rabbit limited room freedom for a while, preferably in an uncarpeted room such as the kitchen. Watch where it defecates. Put some of the fecal matter in the litter box and put the box in the spot that the rabbit used as a toilet area.

In a large room, use two or more litter boxes if necessary. Make sure that they are conveniently located for the rabbit. Remember, untrained rabbits will not travel far to use a litter box, so keep things convenient for them.

3. Never allow the rabbit to wander into other rooms until it is using a litter box. This is where problems will otherwise start, especially if it urinates on a carpet and you don't notice this.

4. Only when the rabbit is using its box should it be allowed into other rooms. Place another litter box in that room and train again. Only by the process of steadily allowing more freedom and training on a *room to room* basis can you hope to really be successful at litter box training.

If you find that your pet starts to establish a latrine area in a room, rather than use its box, you will have to take immediate action. Thoroughly clean and neutralize the soiled area and then place a litter box on the spot. If this fails, you must either cordon off that area of the room or deny the pet access to the room, the latter being the better option. This is very important. Urine (ammonia)-odor molecules can travel some feet from a stained area.

To avoid complications, it is best to keep the rabbit out of the room for a while until all traces of odor have been eliminated by cleaning and the use of odor neutralizers.

This English Lop has a color defined as broken blue cream.

RABBITS AND OTHER PETS

You will no doubt hear of rabbits that are great pals with their owner's dog, cat, or other animal. What is not so well promoted is the number of rabbits and other small pets that are injured, killed, or eaten by their owner's other pets!

You must never assume that a rabbit will get on with other animals, especially with those that are its predators in the wild: dogs, cats, ferrets, and snakes. Always supervise introductions. *Never* allow young children to be unsupervised, even for a short time, when the rabbit and other predatory animals are in the same room, or yard.

A rabbit can get on fine with a guinea pig; it will show little interest in a hamster, mouse, or small bird. It could be bitten by a medium to large parrot. If you have a very benign dog, it *may* become your rabbit's pal. Cats will generally avoid large rabbits, but may attack small ones—if only in play.

The same is true of large dogs that get overexcited. Always take a cautious view until you are absolutely confident that your pets are compatible with your rabbit. If you are prepared to work at integrating your rabbit into your daily home life, you will find it to be every bit as worthwhile as a dog, cat or other pet. Sure, there are some problems to cope with, but isn't this true for a number of other household pets?

HANDLING RABBITS

The way you handle your rabbit will be important in determining whether it enjoys being picked up or if it will wriggle and scratch to be free. *Never* pick it up by its ears. Restrain it by placing one hand over the ears and neck, while using the free hand to scoop under its body to brace its weight. It is the feeling of insecurity that prompts a rabbit to wriggle, using its hind feet and claws to rake at your arm.

Once you have a secure hold of the pet, bring it to your chest to provide further support. You can then place one hand around its chest and neck while cradling its rump on your other arm. Once it is familiar with gentle, but secure, handling, you will find that your pet will have no fears at being cradled on its

There are cases where rabbits and dogs get along well in the same household. But usually the two animals do NOT do well together.

The Cashmere Dwarf Lop is a very expensive breed (at least at the time of this writing), but it is a beautiful, sensitive, friendly animal that is a favorite for children.

back so that you can inspect its nails and underbody parts. Ensure that children are taught how to lift a rabbit correctly. Doing so can prevent injury to both the rabbit and the child.

HOUSE RABBIT DO'S AND DON'TS

1. Do prepare carefully for a house rabbit. Consider the drawbacks first. If you think that you can cope with them, you are on the road to successful rabbit ownership.

2. Do not compare a rabbit with other household pets: this will lead to problems. Treat the rabbit as a unique individual.

3. Do check each room that the pet is allowed into for potential dangers.

4. Do not allow rabbits house freedom when an unsupervised young child is nearby. This is posing an unnecessary risk to the welfare of the rabbit.

5. Do be very patient when litter training a rabbit. Litter training is an alien concept for a rabbit's limited intelligence to readily grasp. Never try to discipline a bunny: you will achieve nothing other than to frighten it.

NUTRITION

The rabbit is a herbivorous animal. This means that its diet is composed of all kinds of plant foods: grasses, seeds, plants, vegetables, and fruits, as well as their byproducts. While they are not meat eaters, some foods of high-protein content are beneficial, especially to growing youngsters and breeding females.

Rabbits are very cosmopolitan eaters, which makes it easy for you to supply a range of beneficial items that they will enjoy. Many foods are stocked in your kitchen, so you will never be without something to offer as a treat or beneficial nutrient item. However, *the main part of your rabbit's diet will be the pelleted rabbit food that can be purchased at pet shops.*

FEEDING UTENSILS

You will need a water pot or gravity-fed bottle dispenser, a pot for dry foods, and one for moist foods and/or mashes. Pots should be of the heavy crock type: anything lightweight will be chewed and/or flung around the accommodations.

Automatic water dispensers should be of the best quality. They may otherwise leak at the spout. This author prefers open water dishes because they are a more natural way for a rabbit to drink, though they must be cleaned and replenished each day.

FOOD TYPES

Your rabbit's rations can be divided into two basic types:

Rabbits must have their own clean feeding dish. It should be cleaned out before each use.

Low-in-additive treats for many different small-mammal pets are available in pet shops.

Those that are dry and those that are moist. Dry foods include pelleted rabbit food, various grains, such as oats and maize, seeds, cereal products, toasted bread, dried fruits, and hay. Moist foods comprise all fresh vegetables, fruits, and mash mixtures containing any number of potential ingredients.

FOOD VALUES

Dry foods are very concentrated in their ingredients; moist foods are mainly water. Pelleted rabbit foods are formulated to provide all the essential ingredients for maintaining good health. They should be the staple diet for your pet. They are fortified with necessary vitamins, proteins, and fatty acids.

Their drawback is that they give no psychological variety to the diet, no opportunity to be selective, or to especially enjoy the flavors of fresh foods. For these reasons, you should supply other foods as well as pellets.

Cereal crops are rich in carbohydrates, which are day-to-day energy foods. Seeds vary in their content, some being rich in protein, some in carbohydrates, others a balance between the two.

Fruits and vegetables have low protein, carbohydrate, and fat contents relative to their weight but are rich in vitamins.

PLANNING A BALANCED DIET

The objective of a well-planned diet is to ensure maximum growth and condition, avoiding underweight or obesity. To achieve this is not simply a case of supplying enough food in quantity, but to ensure that it is balanced. A dish full of oats, some table scraps, and a few carrots would not be a balanced diet. Such a regimen would prevent a rabbit from achieving full health and vigor. The rabbit would be more at risk to illness than a pet whose diet was carefully planned.

Pelleted rabbit foods must form part of the diet because they have all of the ingredients known to be of importance to these lagomorphs.

Their protein content will range from 14-20 percent, which is what your pet needs for typical growth, health, and activity. They can be supplied on a free-choice basis, meaning that the food bowl always contains a supply of them.

A selection of other dry foods, such as crushed oats, flaked maize, and bran, can be added to the pellets. Fresh hay provides good fiber content and is always appreciated by rabbits. Alfalfa hay is the dried form of the plant *Medicago sativa,* a member of the pea family.

It is very important that fresh water is always available to your pet, especially when the diet is essentially of dry foods. Without this precious liquid, your rabbit would soon display signs of ill health.

The fresh (moist) food part of the diet can include carrots, celery, kale, cauliflower, turnips, boiled potatoes, apple, and other fruits and vegetables. It can also include fresh grass and wild plants such as dandelion, coltsfoot, clover, chickweed, plantain and many others. But do ensure that no dangerous wild plants are given: if in doubt, leave it out.

Lettuce and cabbage offer little nutritional benefit. An excess can

Your local pet shop will almost certainly have a specialized diet for rabbits. These feeds usually have a complete diet which contains all the necessary nourishment and vitamins. Photo courtesy of Kaytee.

Rawhide Oodles® is a hard chew treat with low fat and high protein. Designed for use with rodents, such treats can have value for rabbits, which share with rodents the characteristic of continuously growing teeth.

cause problems. Never feed any greenfoods to a rabbit under six months of age. Never supply any fresh foods in a sudden glut. The consequence will be scouring: acute diarrhea that may lead to a major problem.

Fresh foods are best supplied in a mixed salad form to provide an interesting choice yet not too much of any one item. Remove uneaten fresh foods so that they have minimum time to sour. Fresh foods are best supplied early in the morning, or in the late afternoon, when the temperature is cooler.

OBESITY

This is a major problem in most pets for the following reasons:

1. They are given too much food, especially proteins and fats, relative to their activity level.

2. They are given too many food treats that are high in protein or fats.

3. They may develop an eating syndrome to compensate for stress created by restrictive living conditions: too much time in a cage or hutch.

4. To overcome obesity, consider the pet's entire feeding regimen and *activity level*. The diet may be fine, it being a case that the rabbit is grossly under-exercised. If this is not the case, reduce the quantity of the meals, especially of pellets and any high protein seeds such as sunflower, and peanut, if these items are supplied free choice. You may have to feed them on a rationed basis.

GNAWING FOODS

The incisor teeth of rabbits grow continually. It is most important that rabbits have access to hard foods on which they can gnaw.

Pellets are one item, but others can be supplied in the form of short bits of fruit tree branches and baked bread that is on the hard side. Failure to keep the teeth in trim will result in the pet being unable to eat correctly. If the teeth become overgrown, you *must* have your vet trim them.

Rabbits seem to enjoy some variety in their diet. Pet shops carry many such treats. Photo courtesy of Kaytee.

COPROPHAGY

It may appear that your rabbit is eating its fecal pellets. This is not so. It is actually eating cecal pellets: foods partially digested and voided at the anus. By being consumed, these food pellets are passed through the digestive system a second time, enabling maximum benefit to be extracted from their nutrients. The process may be compared with the ruminants' regurgitation of food (chewing the cud).

One of the drawbacks to mesh floors is that they deny rabbits the opportunity to benefit from this very natural part of their digestive process. Because of this, it is especially important that pets kept on such floors are supplied a well-balanced diet to compensate for any potential inadequacies.

FOOD STORAGE

The first rule of feeding is that any item not fresh or in "healthy" condition should be thrown out. Moist foods, such as vegetables and fruits, do not stay fresh for long periods of time. Store them in a refrigerator. Uneaten items should be discarded. Fresh crops should be rinsed to remove harmful residual chemicals used in spraying.

Pellets should be stored in a cool, dry, darkened cupboard, or suitable container. Avoid metal bins, which can sweat in hot weather, resulting in condensation that will encourage mold growth. Pellets must never smell moldy, nor should they be crumbly in texture. If they are, they will be unhealthy for your rabbit. The same applies to cereal crops.

Your rabbit can live very well on a pellet diet, but they do enjoy some fresh vegetables like carrots, celery, apples, dandelion, etc. as an *occasional* treat.

Hay should smell fresh, never stale, or with a black-gray powdery appearance inside if it's purchased in bales. Do not store baled hay directly on concrete. Place it on a raised wooden slatted frame so that air can circulate underneath it.

Pellets and cereal crops can be stored for up to six months under ideal conditions. You are better off to purchase no more than a month's supply at a time. This reduces the risk that it could go stale. Purchase rabbit rations, especially those in bulk, only from stores who are obviously diligent in their general hygiene standards.

FEEDING DO'S AND DON'TS

1. Do maintain high standards of cleaning in cages so that there is minimum risk of dirt and fecal contamination of foods.

2. Do not try to economize on your pet's nutrition. Its health and liveliness will be a direct reflection of its diet.

3. Do provide a varied and balanced menu of food items. Rabbits enjoy eating as much as you do—they have their likes and dislikes.

4. Do watch your pet when it is eating. Any change in its appetite could be the first sign of a problem.

5. Do not feed vitamin or other supplements if a balanced diet is already being eaten and the rabbit is in good health. Excess vitamins can be as harmful as a lack of them. If in doubt, consult your vet.

A show–quality Belgian hare. This is a beautiful rabbit. Unfortunately, a rabbit's conformation to a show standard does not make it a more friendly and peaceful pet.

BREEDING & EXHIBITION

This small handbook was written for the first-time rabbit owner, so breeding and exhibition are discussed only at basic primer level. If your rabbit is a pet, and you have no great desire to become a serious breeder, there is no benefit at all in ever letting your female have a litter of babies.

Indeed, you will merely be contributing to the overpopulation of rabbits resulting from pet owners having unwanted litters, or those with the mistaken belief that one or two litters will be good for the female. They will not. Pets are best neutered—they will make better companions, males especially.

THE POTENTIAL BREEDER

If you think you would like to be a breeder, your strategy should be to gain experience with neutered pets of the breed that you like.

Visit shows and gather information on your breed. Maybe you could enter your bunny in pet classes at exhibitions.

Good planning is essential for the success of your breeding program. Equipment, time, and, of course, the price of stock in your breed must be carefully considered. To start with less than top-quality rabbits makes no sense: it will lead only to disappointment. It costs no more to feed and care for top stock than to rear mediocre examples. Your ongoing costs will far exceed initial purchase outlay, so bear this in mind.

BREEDING FACTS

Sexing: Very young rabbits are difficult to sex until they are three or more months old. Gently place the rabbit on its back in the palm of your hand and inspect the genital area using your free hand. The vagina of the female is closer to the anus than is the penis of the male. By applying gentle pressure on either side of the genital opening, it is possible to see the membrane covering the vagina of the female—the penis being more obvious. The female has nipples, which the male does

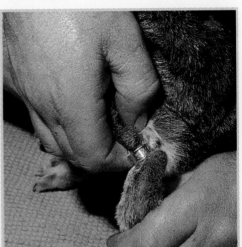

Rabbits can be tagged for positive identification. Many rabbits look alike, and they might be mixed up at a show unless they are properly tagged for identification.

not have. The more mature rabbit is easier to sex, the scrotal sacs of the male being evident on either side of the anus.

Breeding Age: The small and dwarf breeds can be sexually mature as early as 14 weeks of age, the larger breeds taking a longer time. However, breeding very young females has little merit. They should be allowed to mature physically. A small breed should be 6 months old before being bred, a large one about 12 months or a little more.

Litters Per Year: A rabbit may be capable of about seven litters per year. This is not recommended, two to four being ample for any female.

Estrus Cycle: The female rabbit cycle is about 16 days: she will accept the male on about 14 of these days and is generally described as an induced ovulator. This means the presence of a male is sufficient to induce her to commence shedding eggs in readiness for fertilization by the male.

Mating Procedure: The female is taken to the male's accommodations. If she appears very aggressive toward his advances, remove her and try again the next day. If a mating is observed, remove her and repeat the mating within 24 hours: this maximizes litter size. Thereafter, place her back in her own home.

Gestation Period: This is the time between fertilization of the eggs and kindling (the birth of the babies). It is within the range of 28-33 days, 31 being typical.

Litter Size: This varies, depending upon the breed. In small breeds, a typical litter would be four to six, in large breeds five to eight. The young are born naked, deaf, and blind, but development is rapid. The fur starts showing through by the fourth day. Ears and eyes open by about the ninth day. The youngsters start to leave the nest by 17-21 days of age.

Weaning: This is the time when the babies are eating solid foods

Rabbits are prolific breeders; and if kept in free association, they can produce seven litters per year!

A pair of Netherland Dwarfs mating.

and able to live independently of their mother. It ranges from four to eight weeks, depending on the size of the litter and other care factors. Baby rabbits are extremely susceptible to problems when they are about four to six weeks old unless conditions are excellent. Remember that they should not be fed greenfoods. A young rabbit should not go to its new home before the age of eight weeks.

Longevity: Six to eight years is the average, over this a bonus.

RABBIT EXHIBITIONS

Rabbit shows are the shop window to the entire rabbit hobby. At a large show, you will see just about every rabbit breed in your country, and most of the color varieties in them as well. There are booths displaying the latest in rabbit equipment, appliances, and everything else that could conceivably be sold to a rabbit lover.

Apart from the actual thrill of competition, you will meet many breeders and no doubt strike up friendships that can endure the rest of your life. Rabbit exhibitions can become addictive—and you do not have to be an exhibitor to be a regular showgoer. Many owners go just for the fun of it and to keep in touch with all that's happening in the hobby.

GETTING INVOLVED

If you wish to become involved with the show side of the hobby, you should join your national association. In the US, young people (ages 9 to 19) can also join 4-H, which has an excellent rabbit program.

The national association issues standards of perfection for each of the breeds, and most breeds also have their own club. Rabbits are judged by comparing them against each other, and how they compare with the standard. The associations produce their own magazines, in which all upcoming shows are announced—as well as articles on rabbit keeping.

Shows may be cooped, which means that cages are provided for exhibitors, or are carry case, which means that you keep your bunny in its carry case and take the pet to the judge's table when called. The large shows will be cooped. They are divided into many classes, the number being determined by the size of the show. Each breed has age, color, and sex classes. Additionally, there are normally classes for pet owners.

An exhibition rabbit must be registered. In the US, it carries a tattooed ID number in its left ear; in the UK, it will have a legband that can only be fitted when the rabbit is a youngster. ID marks are not needed for pet classes.

Class winners in each variety progress to compete for Best and Best Opposite Sex for the variety. They will then compete for Best and Best Opposite Sex

A newborn rabbit is born helpless and dependent upon his mother. Hares are born furred, with their eyes open, and are capable of running within a few minutes after birth.

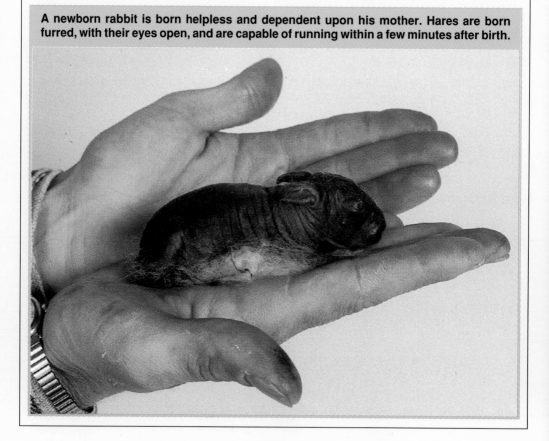

A Checkered Giant eight days old.

for each breed. The winners ultimately compete for the coveted Best in Show award.

There are many rules and regulations that govern rabbit shows. You need not fear them because show secretaries and exhibitor/breeders in your area are really helpful to beginners. But it is best if you visit a few shows first: you will see how things are done.

What you will come to appreciate above all else is that there is a world of difference between the average pet rabbit and the ones that are winning at shows. They will display magnificent condition, gorgeous coats, and superb color patterns. They will excite your imagination.

BREEDING DO'S AND DON'TS

1. Do not allow pet rabbits to breed: this is of no benefit to them, to you, or the hobby.

2. Do consider very carefully all of the problems inherent with breeding before you commit to a breeding program.

3. Do not breed other than quality stock: it will achieve nothing for you.

4. Do maintain the highest of hygiene standards when rearing babies. They quickly succumb to illness if conditions are not excellent.

HEALTH

Rabbits are very hardy little mammals. If they become ill, it is often due to a breakdown in husbandry management. You are not advised to try and diagnose and/or treat an unwell rabbit. Even an experienced breeder would be wise to leave this vital subject to his veterinarian.

Very often, pet owners want instant diagnosis and a cure-all for a problem once it becomes apparent. To avoid a vet bill, they will try and diagnose the condition by reference to a book.

It is not that simple. An incorrect diagnosis and treatment can be counterproductive, even fatal, to your pet.

A book of this size cannot begin to describe the clinical signs of the many diseases, how they are confirmed by laboratory techniques, what treatments should be given, for how long, and what the risks are. What it *can* do is to advise you about how to avoid problems in the first place. This is the best way that you can keep those vet bills to a minimum!

WHAT YOU SHOULD KNOW ABOUT ILL HEALTH

As a concerned owner, the following subjects are the ones in which you should develop an in-depth knowledge. They form the platform of all sound husbandry techniques for any animal.

PRECURSORS OF ILL HEALTH

The potential number of diseases and ailments that can afflict your pet are legion. From a young age, your rabbit begins building an immunity to many of them. Should a given bacterium, virus, or fungus arrive near your pet, its immune system will be capable of defending the rabbit against it—as long as the rabbit is in good health.

Should it not do so because the pathogenic attack is overwhelmingly strong, modern drugs from your veterinarian will normally effect a remedy if they are given as soon as the problem is evident and diagnosed by the vet.

If a rabbit is not in good health when pathogens strike, its immune system will be less effective. It will more rapidly succumb to the pathogen(s). This situation will accelerate if its living conditions favor a rapid increase in pathogenic colonization. Anything that suppresses the immune system will also favor and increase the rate of health deterioration.

Precursors of ill health include any combination of the following. Use the list as a one-by-one checklist.

Hygiene: Unclean, cracked, or chipped feeding appliances; dirty floors; unclean cage bars; dirty nestbox; difficult-to-clean cages

Opposite: **A perfectly healthy Giant Angora. A healthy rabbit looks healthy and eats well. Your pet rabbit should be under constant observation for any deviation in eating or behavioral patterns.**

(unprotected surfaces);and generally dirty conditions around the cage.

Food: Non-fresh foods; dirty water; incorrectly stored foods; and stale and soured foods left in the cage.

Environment: Lack of ventilation; inadequate temperature control; excessive humidity; and ineffective fly/parasite control.

Stress: Overcrowding; bullying; sudden frights; inadequate diet; excessive breeding of a female; breeding from stock that is not in sound condition; lack of space; lack of exercise; and boredom.

General Safeguards: Not washing hands before handling pets; lack of clean protective clothing (in breeding rooms); handling pets after gardening; no isolation/quarantine facility; (applicable to breeders); and visiting establishments that keep rabbits and/or other animals under less-than-adequate sanitary conditions.

Preventive management means that each of the items listed should be constantly under review: the one(s) that you overlook may be the very one(s) that enable pathogens to establish themselves.

HOW PATHOGENS REACH YOUR PET

Disease organisms do not start in or near your rabbit. They are ever present in the atmosphere and gain access to your pet, which becomes a home and breeding ground to them, in any of the following ways.

English Lops require cleaner surroundings than do most other rabbits because their ears are almost always touching the floor.

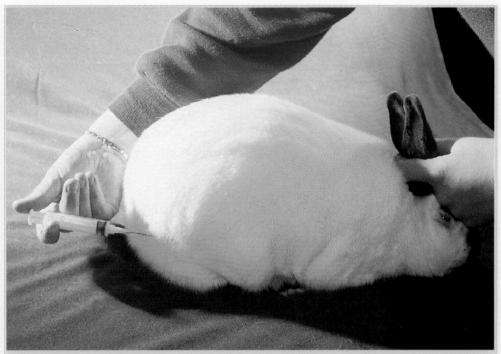

When in doubt of your rabbit's health, take it to your local vet. Rabbits can be vaccinated against many diseases.

1. Airborne pathogens, or their eggs/spores, are blown into your home.

2. Flies and other intermediate hosts act as carriers. They transfer the pathogens to food, cage surfaces, and elsewhere.

3. They are introduced by other pets, especially other rabbits, that you may acquire, but that seem healthy at the time.

4. They are introduced by you or visitors who have picked them up on their clothing/hands when visiting pet shops, vets, farms, rabbitries, or even rabbit shows. Pathogens are everywhere.

5. They are introduced via tainted foods, or foods that have not been correctly stored (moldy pellets, grain, hay).

Once on your property, and rabbit, pathogens will multiply if conditions favor them. They will transfer, by proximal or direct contact, to other rabbits that you may have. The spores of some pathogens, once established, can persist for weeks, even months, after the problem, or disease they created, has been overcome.

RECOGNIZING ILL HEALTH

It is not difficult to spot obvious signs, such as weeping eyes, runny nose, and so on. But diseases may not always display external signs, or may do so only when they reach advanced stages. In these instances, the only early visual warning that you may notice will be changes in your pet's patterns of behavior. Watch for the following:

1. Disinterest in food, especially favored items.

2. Undue lethargy and sleeping.

3. Seeking a quiet refuge during periods that would normally be active times—when seeing you approach for example.

4. Obvious reluctance (or pain) to being handled.

5. Difficulty in, or noisy, breathing. Panting.

6. Unusual movements such as twirling and uncontrolled twitching, sudden darting movements, and exhaustion.

7. Excessive thirst or eating.

8. Repeated scratching or vomiting.

9. Difficulty in defecating or urinating.

10. Difficulty, or obvious pain, when moving about.

The symptoms that you see will determine your course of action. For example, a weeping eye, or nose, may be no more than a minor chill. A rabbit that has been running around on a warm day may breath heavier than normal, or be more tired than usual.

During hot weather, a rabbit may eat somewhat less than usual, and drink more. It may scratch now and then. These are all normal situations not

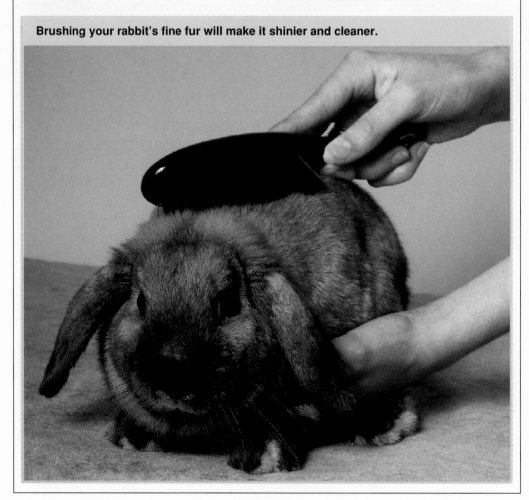

Brushing your rabbit's fine fur will make it shinier and cleaner.

Mini Lops, like the one shown here, make excellent pets.

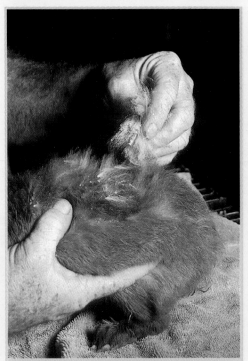

This rabbit is suffering from skin mange and has lost a considerable amount of fur. Such a condition warrants veterinary attention.

thoroughly clean) or move your rabbit's cage to a dry, warm (a few degrees higher than its normal environment), quiet area away from children and general noise and activity.

Next, inspect the rabbit's cage for signs of diarrhea, blood, or anything else that might have a bearing on the current problem.

Gather samples (a few) of the rabbit's fecal matter. Place them in a suitable container. Before consulting your vet, make a few notes on the situation so that nothing slips your mind.

1. What prompted you to decide that the rabbit was unwell?

2. How many hours ago was this?

indicative of any pending problem. Once clinical and behavioral signs are seen together, and if they persist more than 36 hours, then it is the time to take a more serious view of them.

REACTING TO ILL HEALTH

Having decided that your rabbit is not well, act quickly—time is now the enemy. Do not ignore minor conditions such as colds or small cuts, because if they are not treated quickly they may result in secondary conditions or infections that are far more serious and difficult to treat.

Your first action is to isolate the pet from all other animals. Either place it in a cage kept specially for sick pets (be very sure this cage is

Your rabbit's fur should always be soft, shiny and without lumps or knots. During your petting process, observe the health of your rabbit's coat.

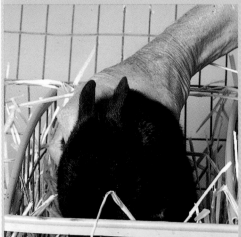

3. Over what period of time has the condition deteriorated, and in what ways?

4. Are other pets in the home ill? Do you know their problem?

5. Has your rabbit (or other pets) had any recent illness?

6. Is there any chance that the rabbit could have eaten some poisonous or dangerous chemical?

You should reflect on all recent happenings that could have created the problem. Your be given emergency advice, pending on your being able to visit the clinic. Fecal samples should be placed in a container and stored the refrigerator, not the freezer.

CORRECTING PROBLEMS

Once an illness has been diagnosed and is being treated, you *must* review all of your husbandry practices to try and avoid history repeating itself. Begin by conducting a total

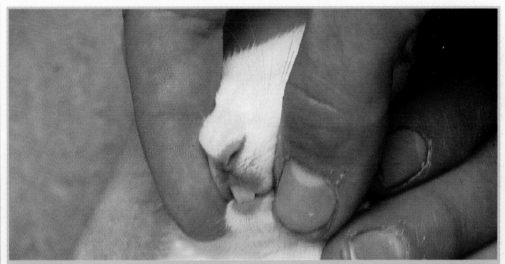

If a rabbit's teeth are not properly aligned, the correct gnawing action to wear them down is lacking; and the teeth will continue to grow.

vet will appreciate all information, including the rabbit's diet, how old it is, how long you have owned it, and from where it was purchased, if this was recently.

Now contact the vet. If you live within easy reach of your veterinarian, and the problem sounds worrisome, the vet will request that you bring the rabbit to the clinic for examination. If you are a long way from the vet and cannot go that day, you will cleaning operation. Dispose of all bedding, floor covering, and chipped or cracked feeding utensils. This is especially important when treating for lice, fleas, and other ectoparasites.

Wooden hutches are often neglected in respect to their upkeep. Internal surfaces should be painted each year after very thorough disinfecting. If the illness was fungal in nature, you will need appropriate treatments from your vet for cleaning. Household disinfectants will rarely be effective. Bleach is a better choice.

If you have a number of rabbits and any die without displaying obvious clinical signs, it is worthwhile having the vet conduct a postmortem. This may reveal the causal organism and better enable you to take whatever steps are needed to prevent further spread or reinfection.

TREATMENTS

There is an ever growing list of excellent modern drugs that your vet can use for treating rabbits. It is important that you follow instructions and complete the treatments that are prescribed. Drugs have a very definite shelf life and must also be stored correctly if they are to retain their efficacy.

Never assume that increasing the amounts will increase their effectiveness: this can be dangerous logic. Nor should you use unprescribed drugs indiscriminately. This can be lethal. They may destroy vital beneficial bacteria in the gut of the rabbit, depleting it of essential vitamins at a very critical time.

If you follow the advice given in this chapter, you will experience few problems that are not readily remedied.

Understanding and applying sound husbandry techniques really is the cornerstone to success. Veterinary treatments are merely short-term methods to cope with problems. They do not prevent a recurrence; good husbandry invariably does.

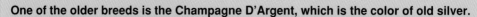

One of the older breeds is the Champagne D'Argent, which is the color of old silver.

RABBIT BREEDS

There are well over 100 rabbit breeds recognized around the world. Of them, at least 45 have show standards in the US, and 48 have show standards in Britain. These numbers are steadily increasing. In this chapter, we will look at a number of the very popular breeds, as well as some of those that are less seen. Descriptions are necessarily brief. You can refer to your national association's official standards for a detailed description.

WHAT MAKES A BREED?

With a few notable exceptions, most rabbit breeds look broadly similar. Whereas in dogs each breed is of a very distinct conformation, this is far less so in rabbits. Here, other criteria are used to define a breed. They may be based on fur type, color, pattern, ear type, size, or a combination of these features. Within many of the breeds, there will be color varieties.

In this chapter, for your ease of reference, the breeds are grouped by size: small, medium, and large. This enables you to review the breeds of the size that you feel would be best suited to your needs. Using this method, there are about 17 small breeds (of which 10 might be considered mini breeds or dwarfs), 27 medium breeds, and 22 large breeds. Over half of them are discussed in this chapter.

Following the name of the breed, you will see its upper weight limit in the US, fur type, and generally accepted country of origin. Weight limits in Britain may be higher or lower in some breeds. Suggested similar alternatives are given in a number of instances.

SMALL BREEDS—2.5-6.5 LBS. (1.1-2.9KG)

Whether as house pets, or breeding/show candidates, the small breeds have become the most popular group to own. They display a range of fur, color, and pattern types. They are low cost to house and maintain.

Netherland Dwarf: 2.5 lbs. (1.1kg); short smooth fur; Great Britain

The popular blue Netherland Dwarf.

A pair of blue-eyed white Netherland Dwarfs.

Developed in Britain and Europe during the 19th century, the Netherland is the most popular breed in the US. Its color range and patterns are greater than in any other breed: black, blue, orange, white, agouti, Himalayan, whatever your choice, there is probably a Netherland in it. Choose with care because these dwarfs may suffer from incorrect tooth alignment. Poorly bred individuals may have tempers as short as their size.

Alternatives, but far less popular, would be the Polish, Britannia Petite, and the beautiful dark eye-rimmed white Dwarf Hotot, which is a miniature of the much larger Hotot.

Jersey Wooly: 3.5 lbs. (1.6kg); wooly fur; US

Developed during the 1970s from crosses between Angoras and dwarf breeds, the Jersey sports erect ears and a dense wooly coat that gives it a larger than true-size appearance. Available in a range of colors, it is a welcome addition to the breeds.

The Holland Lop is not always available as a pet. Your pet shop usually can order any breed in any color. Ask them!

Regular grooming is a necessity with this breed. A long-eared alternative would be the American Fuzzy Lop, which was produced using the Jersey Wooly.

Holland Lop: 4 lbs. (1.8kg); fine, dense, glossy fur; Holland

This chunky bundle arrived in the US during the mid–1970s and is now one of the most popular breeds. Available in a range of colors and patterns, it has a domed forehead, manageable lop ears, and a really cute appearance. No wonder kids just love them. A small dewlap is permissible in does. The American Fuzzy Lop, the Mini (Dwarf), and Cashmere Lop (Britain), would be the obvious alternatives.

Mini Rex: 4.5 lbs. (2kg); dense velvet-like fur; US

Developed in Texas by Mona Berryhill by crossing a small Rex with a Netherland dwarf, and by other breeders using imports and Rexes. The Mini Rex is unusual in that it displays none of the typical dwarf breed's head features. Being a diminutive version of its larger ancestor, it is aptly named. The prime feature is, of course, a gorgeous, plush velvet-like coat that has to be felt to be appreciated.

There are about 14 self (the same all over) colors, as well as broken patterns, which are spots and patches of color on a white background. The Rex is a fuss-free breed with a wonderful temperament, so it is no surprise to find that it has gained tremendous popularity, both as a pet and an exhibition rabbit.

Himalayan: 4.5 lbs. (2kg); short, fine, glossy fur; origin uncertain

Generally regarded as being of Asiatic origin (possibly China), the Himalayan is one of the oldest established breeds. It is named for its pointed color pattern, which is either black or blue on a pure white background. The color appears on the points: nose, ears, feet, and tail. You should not confuse the true Himalayan breed with the many other breeds that may display the pointed pattern as a variety: the pattern was transferred to these breeds through selective breeding. The Himalayan is a small, sleek breed with a famed tranquil temperament. It is not as

A blue fawn tri-colored Mini Rex.

Above: A magnificent pair of matched Himalayan rabbits. They don't come from the Himalayas, they just have the color of Himalayan cats. *Below:* The Dutch breed was developed in Holland and reaches about five pounds in weight.

popular as it was in past years, but it remains a magnificent breed that will always be well supported.

Alternatives would be those like the Mini Rex and Netherland Dwarf, which are small and are seen with the Himalayan pattern.

Dutch: 5 lbs. (2.5kg); short, dense, sleek fur; Belgium

This breed was developed in England during the late 1890s by Fred Copeman from stock that arrived regularly from Ostend. The Ostend stock was of Dwarf Brabancon type—white with some black markings. The resulting breed was named "Dutch" in England, even before the breed was firmly established. It is possible that the breed was named for the black-and-white clothing worn by the ladies of

Holland. The Dutch has become the most well-recognized rabbit in the world.

It is bicolored, with the front half of the body, rear feet, and an inverted "V" on the face being white, the rest of the body, ears, and cheeks being one of a number of different colors. They include black, blue, gray (agouti), chocolate, yellow, or tortoiseshell. Producing well-marked individuals is extremely difficult, many being mismarked. The Dutch should be a very docile bunny. In spite of the many excellent new small breeds, the Dutch remains very popular. It is thoroughly deserving of its popular standing. There is no obvious alternative to the Dutch, other than in size.

Tan: 6 lbs. (2.7kg); short, dense, glossy fur; Great Britain

The Tan breed originated in the U.K. and reaches about six pounds in weight.

Developed on an English estate by crossing wild rabbits with the Dutch in the late 1800s. It was originally black and tan, but today there are blue, chocolate and lilac varieties. The body is colored, with the tan being on the underparts, throat, eye-rings, and

The Florida White was developed mainly to be used for research.

inner ears. A very striking rabbit with beautiful glossy fur. A popular show breed. An alternative, but with black-and-silver color, would be the Silver Marten.

Florida White: 6 lbs. (2.7kg); short, sleek fur; US

Developed in Florida as a small meat and laboratory breed from crosses involving the Dutch, Polish, and New Zealand White. The eyes are pink. Not a visually stunning breed but one that enjoys a good following. Alternatives: Dwarf Hotot, Polish, Netherland Dwarf, Britannia Petite, and Mini Rex.

MEDIUM BREEDS—6.5- 9.5 LBS. (2.9-4.3KG)

These breeds make ideal house or outbuilding pets, as they are moderate in their housing needs and in their upkeep. As a weight group, there are nearly twice as many recognized breeds in Great Britain as there are in the US. But the most popular are seen in both countries.

Mini Lop: 6.5 lbs. (2.9kg); short, dense, sleek fur; Holland

Known as the Dwarf Lop in Britain, where it is a smaller

Clare Gilroy with her Dwarf Lop.

The Havana breed originally was gorgeous chocolate brown, the color of the wrapper on a fine Havana cigar.

named for the cigar. Today, there are black and blue varieties as well. Havanas have enjoyed a select following in exhibition circles since the early years of this century and have been used in the creation of a number of breeds in which chocolate was a desired color. They have a very typical rabbit shape and no special management considerations—such as flop ears or long coats—to worry about.

Chinchilla: 7.5 lbs. (3.3kg); fine, dense, wavy fur; France

A pair of Standard Chinchilla rabbits.

breed. It is a miniature version of the large French Lop. The crown is raised in profile. The muzzle displays a smooth curve to the nose. This is a cute-looking bunny, which, together with its diminutive size, accounts for its tremendous popularity.

It is available in a wide range of colors and patterns to suit any preference. Its obvious alternatives would be the Holland and Fuzzy Lops, as well as its much larger ancestor, the French Lop.

Havana: 6.5 lbs. (2.9kg); medium, dense, sleek fur; Holland

This breed's main feature is its superb glossy coat. The Havana was originally a dark chocolate,

Based on the original French breed, a number of chinchilla breeds have been produced in Europe, the US, and elsewhere. Here we will discuss the Standard

Chinchilla. The prime feature is, of course, the fur named for the rodent. When brushed against its lie, there should be bands of slate blue, pearl, black, then light blue, tipped with black.

The breed was developed as a fur and meat breed in the early 1900s. It soon became a popular show and pet breed but has since lost its former support as a pet due to the competition from smaller, more brightly colored and patterned breeds. The alternative, if you like large breeds, would be the Giant Chinchilla, which can weigh in at over 13 lbs. (5.9+kg).

English Angora: 7.5 lbs. (3.4kg); long, silky, wooly fur; Great Britain

The true origins of this breed are unknown. Some say it was

A pair of Satin Angoras.

developed in Turkey; others believe that the mutation was first established in Great Britain, then taken to mainland Europe. There are three Angora breeds, the English being the smallest. It has a full coat of wool that extends to fringes on the ears. The fringes distinguish it from the French breed, which is larger and has no ear furnishings. The Giant Angora

is a much larger version of the English.

While the English is a magnificent rabbit, its long profuse coat makes it better suited to the serious hobbyist who is prepared to spend time grooming. If not, the coat will quickly become an unkempt tangle of mats. Problems can be created by hair being swallowed and forming hairballs in the rabbit's stomach.

English Spot: 8 lbs. (3.6kg); dense, short, sleek fur; Great Britain

A pair of English Spots.

This very old breed was standardized as long ago as 1891. Many fanciers regard it as the supreme exhibition rabbit because perfection is so difficult to achieve in the breed. Most offspring in a litter fall well short of the high standard needed.

The English is characterized by the solid line of color running down the back, and the chain of spots on the flanks, coupled with the dark ears, butterfly smut and dark eye-ring, all on a white background. Available colors are black, blue, chocolate, gold, gray,

Harlequins, Japanese and Magpie. This breed averages a little over nine pounds in weight.

lilac, and tortoiseshell. It has always been a popular pet and continues to attract new followers in every generation. Alternatives would be the American Checkered Giant or the Rhinelander. Each has a similar pattern.

Harlequin: 9.5 lbs. (4.3kg); short, dense, sleek fur; France

Originally very much larger, the Harlequin's alternating color pattern is very difficult to produce to exhibition standard. Not as popular as in former years, good examples are stunningly attractive.

If the colors of black, blue, chocolate, or lilac are combined with golden-orange or fawn, they are termed Japanese. If they appear with white, they are termed Magpie. Rex and astrex (curly) coats are also seen in this breed.

Silver Marten: 9.5 lbs. (4.3kg); short, dense, glossy fur; Anglo-German

Known in Great Britain as the Silver Fox, for which it was

The Silver Marten.

named. It was originally black with white underparts, and silver tipping to the hairs of the lower half of the body. Today, there are blue, chocolate, and sable varieties. This is a very imposing rabbit.

It is basically a black and tan, with the tan being replaced by white. Not as popular a pet as in former years, it retains a strong group of dedicated exhibitor/breeders.

The Belgian Hare reaches almost ten pounds in weight.

Belgian Hare: 9.5 lbs. (4.3kg); short, dense, sleek fur; Belgium
Named for its color, which resembles that of a hare. The original breed underwent a complete change in type and color after it was exported to Great Britain in about 1874. The resulting graceful breed that we see today became immensely popular as a show rabbit. It was largely responsible for making domestic rabbit keeping popular in the US. Today, this elegant, racy breed is no longer very popular. Its historical importance is largely unknown by hobby newcomers. Color is a rich shade of red with black flecking. Its high stance and speed mean it needs generously sized housing.

LARGE BREEDS—10 LBS. (4.5KG) AND OVER

All of these breeds will need very spacious accommodations and will be more costly to feed. If you like "big," these are the breeds for you. They are not the ideal choice for the average first-time pet owner. American owners have a wider choice in this weight category than do those rabbit keepers in Great Britain.

English Lop: 10+ lbs. (4.5+kg); short, dense fur; Great Britain
Very different from the French Lop, this breed sports enormously long ears—in excess of 26 in. in some individuals. It is regarded as being the oldest of the rabbit breeds and is often referred to as the King of the Fancy, although

The English Lop's ears can be the source of problems unless they are well cared for.

some see it as an abomination of what a rabbit is all about. The modern English Lop is a much smaller rabbit than it was at its height of popularity in the early 1900s.

It comes in a range of colors and patterns, but the ears are the all-important feature. The English Lop is not the ideal choice for a

The Californian is an invention of the Americans. It is popular as a show exhibit and as a pet.

pet because those dangling ears can be the source of problems unless they are well cared for. Much more popular are the mini lops, whose ears are proportionately smaller.

Californian: 10.5 lbs. (4.8kg); short, dense fur; US

Developed in the 1920s by crossings of the Himalayan, Chinchilla, and New Zealand White. It looks rather like a large Himalayan with reduced color on the nose. It is black on white only in the US, but brown is accepted in Great Britain. Although originally bred for meat and pelt, it enjoys great popularity as a show exhibit and as a pet. Like most large breeds, it has a benign disposition.

Rex: 10.5 lbs. (4.8kg); short, velvet-like fur; France

The original rex rabbits of the early 1900s, known as Castorrex (King of the Beavers), hardly compare with today's gorgeous examples. Indeed, they were dubbed "wrecks" in Great Britain and the US when they were first introduced during the 1920s. However, breeders, recognizing their potential, started to improve both the coat and the body type. Today this majestic breed truly deserves its regal name.

The Rex grows to over ten pounds. It originated in France.

The Satin breed of rabbit can reach 11 pounds in weight.

Satin: 11 lbs. (5kg); dense, fine, soft lustrous fur; US

This breed resulted from a mutation that appeared in the Havana sometime in the 1930s. The mutation was unacceptable in the Havana, so the Satin became a breed unto itself. Since then it has gained considerable popularity. The satin gene has been transferred to many other breeds. Available in a range of colors and patterns, the Satin's shiny, silky fur always commands attention.

Palomino 11 lbs. (5kg); short, dense, sleek fur; US

Originally called the Washingtonian, this breed was developed during the 1950s. It has built up solid support as an exhibition breed. Two colors are available: golden and lynx. The underside of the tail, belly, foot pads, and jaws are a light cream; the rest of the body has a golden color over the cream underfur. The lynx is a medium pearl-gray blending to orange over a cream underfur.

The Palomino comes in two beautiful color varieties: golden and lynx.

The New Zealand breed can reach twelve pounds in weight.

New Zealand: 12 lbs. (5.4kg); short, dense fur; US

Developed in various parts of the US during the early 1900s, the original New Zealand was red. Today it is also available in black and white, with a blue version having been developed in Great Britain. This large rabbit retains a strong following, though its size limits its pet popularity. It has been used to develop numerous other breeds.

Checkered Giant: 12+lbs. (5.4+kg); short, dense, glossy fur; US

Although this breed was imported from Germany in 1910, the American version is now different from its ancestor. In looks, it resembles the English Spot, but lacks the chain of spots on its flanks. They are replaced by two spots, or groups of them. The Checkered Giant is a popular show exhibit. Obvious alternatives are the English Spot and the Rhinelander.

Flemish Giant: 15+ lbs. (6.75+kg); short, sleek fur; Belgium

A very old breed dating back to the 19th century. The English version is lighter than its American cousin. A dewlap is seen in does. Colors include black, blue, fawn, gray, sandy,

The Flemish Giant is a very large and heavy-boned rabbit. It reaches fifteen pounds in weight.

Above: The Flemish Giant. *Below:* The Jersey Wooly.

and white. Alternatives include the even larger British Giant, the pure frosty-white Blanc De Bouscat, or the lighter Beveren.

BREEDS GROUPED BY DISTINCTIVE FEATURES

Lop-eared breeds: English Lop, French Lop, Mini (Dwarf) Lop, Holland Lop, American Fuzzy Lop

Short-eared breeds: Netherland Dwarf, Britannia Petite, Polish, Dwarf Hotot

Woolly (longhaired) breeds: English Angora, French Angora, Giant Angora, Satin Angora, American Fuzzy Lop, Jersey Wooly

Rex coat: Rex and Mini Rex

Satin coat: Satin. Other breeds may feature a satin coat as a variety.

Spotted color pattern: English Spot, Rhinelander, American Checkered Giant, Rex

Pointed pattern: Himalayan and Californian. Many other breeds feature the pattern as a variety.

Checkered pattern: Harlequin

RABBIT ASSOCIATIONS

American Rabbit Breeders Association, Inc. (ARBA):
PO Box 426
Bloomington, Illinois 61702
US

British Rabbit Council
Purfoy House
7 Kirkgate
Newark
Notts, NG24 1AD
England

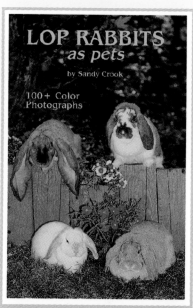